# The Fiology Workbook:
# Your Guide to Financial Independence

By: David Q. Baughier and MK Williams

# fi·ol·o·gy
## /fīˈäləjē/
### noun
### the study of
### Financial Independence

ISBN: 978-1-7330711-0-9 (Paperback)

All content reflects our opinion at a given time and can change as time progresses. All information should be taken as the best advice available at this moment and should not be misconstrued for professional or legal advice.

Cover Design by: Matt Stone | Interior Layout by: Audra King

Printed by Fiology, Inc., in the United States of America.

First printing edition 2019.

Fiology, Inc. 1900 Flintshire Dr. Chesapeake, VA, 23323

https://www.fiology.com/

"*The Fiology Workbook* has more than fifty practical and easy to digest lessons to get you on the path to Financial Independence. Each lesson encourages you to think critically about where you are, where you want to be, and take those next steps to reach your Financial Independence goal."
- **Justin McCurry**, creator of Root of Good

"*The Fiology Workbook: Your Guide to Financial Independence* is the ultimate blueprint for anyone looking to achieve Financial Independence. Learn about the strategies and tactics from some of the thought leaders in the space in 50+ comprehensive lessons. Financial Independence is truly a superpower, you just have to know how to unlock it!"
- **Cody Berman**, founder of Arsenal Discs, creator of Fly to FI and host of The FI Show podcast

"If you've ever heard anything about Financial Independence that made you think that it was out of your reach, you need to dig into this incredible workbook. David has laid out, in a very clear and easy-to-use format, some of the steps you can take to reach your goals. Not only does the workbook give you a host of valuable tips and tricks, it lays out tables that you can use to actually see your progress!"
- **Tinian Crawford**, creator of DIY2FI

"The idea of Financial Independence is thrilling; that good money choices gives us more freedom. But it can also be overwhelming to get started. *The Fiology Workbook: Your Guide to Financial Independence* guides you step by step to start building your best FI life."
- **Jillian Johnsrud**, creator of Montana Money Adventures

"With high-quality curated content spread across over fifty motivating lessons, Fiology is the one-stop-shop for getting started on the journey to Financial Independence! *The Fiology Workbook: Your Guide to Financial Independence* provides the perfect complement to these lessons, creating a structured program that's fun and easy to follow. This is the missing personal finance course I wish I had in college!"
- **Joel**, creator of FI180 and host of the In Love and Money podcast

"This truly is your A-Z guide for achieving Financial Independence. *The Fiology Workbook: Your Guide to Financial Independence* has left no stone unturned. It balances all of the information, questions, and content you need with a digestible and engaging format to keep you going."
- **Nick True**, creator of Mapped Out Money

# TABLE OF CONTENTS

Welcome                                          6-8
From the Founder of Fiology.com

Lesson 1                                           9
What Does Financial Independence Mean
to Me?

Lesson 2                                          11
Why FI?

Lesson 3                                          12
How Much Do I Need?

Lesson 4                                      13 - 19
Milestones of FI

Lesson 5                                          20
The Big Three

Lesson 6                                          22
The Miracle of Compound Interest

Lesson 7                                          23
Where Does All My Money Go?

Lesson 8                                          25
Overcome Debt

Lesson 9                                          27
Retirement Account Basics

Lesson 10                                     28 - 31
Do My Habits Wreak Havoc?

Lesson 11                                         34
Let Our Values Guide Our Decisions

Lesson 12                                         35
The Risks of Financial Independence

Lesson 13                                         37
It Pays to Be Passive

Lesson 14                                         38
The Pension Dimension

Lesson 15                                     39 - 41
Rent or Buy: What's Best for FI?

Lesson 16                                         42
Automatic Financial Independence

Lesson 17                                     43 - 49
Improved Eating Habits: A Recipe for
Financial Independence

Lesson 18                                         50
Kids and Money

Lesson 19                                         52
Don't Evade Tax Knowledge

Lesson 20                                         53
Geoarbitrage

Lesson 21                                     54 - 55
The Secret of FI

Lesson 22                                         56
Higher Education: To Pay or Not to Pay?

Lesson 23                                         58
Should You Pay Off Your Mortgage?

Lesson 24                                         59
Net Worth ≠ Net Happiness

Lesson 25                                         60
You "Can-Do" It Yourself!

Lesson 26                                         61
Withdrawing Funds Before Age 59½

Lesson 27                                         63
Mindfulness

# TABLE OF CONTENTS

Lesson 28
Join Forces for FI ... 64

Lesson 42
Opportunity Costs ... 86

Lesson 29
Cut the Cords That Tie Us Down ... 65

Lesson 43
FI-losophy - Stoicism ... 87

Lesson 30
The FI-brary ... 66

Lesson 44
Sequence of Returns Risk ... 89

Lesson 31
Don't Cell Yourself Short ... 67

Lesson 45
Real Estate Investment Trusts ... 90 - 91

Lesson 32
Whole, Term, or No Life Insurance? ... 68

Lesson 46
One More Year Syndrome ... 92

Lesson 33
Health Insurance ... 69

Lesson 47
Dream Big ... 93

Lesson 34
Reinforce FI with Rentals ... 71

Lesson 48
Caring for Aging Parents ... 94 - 95

Lesson 35
Travel Reward Yourself ... 72

Lesson 49
Social Security ... 96

Lesson 36
Decluttering the Home and Self ... 73 - 78

Lesson 50
The Dynamic Journey ... 97

Lesson 37
Car Buying While Driving Towards FI ... 80 - 81

Lesson 51
Living the FI Life ... 98

Lesson 38
The Prenup Proposal ... 82

Lesson 52
FI-vangelism ... 99

Lesson 39
Side Hustle Up! ... 83

Notes ... 100

Lesson 40
FI with Friends ... 84

Lesson 41
Who is your FI Mentor? ... 85

# Welcome to Fiology!

Congratulations on your decision to achieve Financial Independence. Your future self and family will thank you!

In the simplest terms, you become Financially Independent when your accumulated assets provide income that meets your planned living expenses. Once you've met that mark, you have the option to no longer work a job for pay.

We are only on this planet for a short amount of time. Your choice to achieve Financial Independence means you've decided you don't agree with the traditional life script. Working until you are 65 and retiring to enjoy the last third of your life isn't going to cut it. You want more. You want to take as much control of your future as practically possible. Achieving Financial Independence gives you that control. Even if you start this journey later in life than expected, you will be far better off in the future for committing to it.

As anyone who has been a victim of downsizing, unfortunate circumstance, or simply bad luck knows, life has a way of presenting obstacles. These distractions will factor into our progress toward Financial Independence. Even after we reach our magic number, we are not immune to life's tough times. Being Financially Independent does mean, however, that we weather the storms better when those difficulties arrive.

We all come to this point at different stages of our lives. We have different beliefs, habits, incomes, desires, and skills.

Yet every person on the Financial Independence journey shares a willingness to test the bounds of their understanding and to take action to achieve their goals. The math of Financial Independence is fairly straightforward, but your journey will be anything but simple. You will learn more about yourself and the world around you. You will use this knowledge to design and experience the life you know is right for you.

While this guide will help you explore the critical concepts of Financial Independence, don't forget that there is no "official" right way to achieve Financial Independence. There is simply your way. Fiology, and the content that supports it, will provide methods and justification from the personal knowledge and experience of people walking the Financial Independence path. What they share, while valuable, may not be what you choose to focus on to get you to where you want to go. Learn from it. Understand that it is an option to consider, nothing more.

This is your journey. You will explore your mindset, your habits, your decision-making processes, your own personal philosophy, your happiness, and your beliefs. These factors, at first glance, appear to have little to do with making money. You will discover just how important these factors become in achieving Financial Independence. Do not neglect these concepts.

There is a reason you've chosen to achieve Financial Independence. It isn't because you want to log in to your bank account every day and see a number with a lot of commas. It is what that net worth affords you that's motivating. You may want to spend more time with family, travel, or pursue a hobby. If you remain locked into the traditional script of working a job that continually pulls you away from these fulfilling endeavors, you may not have the time and energy.

Along this journey you will discover others like you, who see the world differently than most. We will help nurture your journey. It is in our nature to spread the message of Financial Independence and serve as a mentor for anyone who truly wants to achieve it. You have the ability to shape your future for the better. Take ownership and do what it takes to discover and live your best life. Fiology and those who support it will be here to provide knowledge and encouragement along the way.

## How to Use This Guide

This guide is designed as a companion for the lessons section of the fiology.com website. Go to fiology.com now and enroll in the free weekly lessons. Each week, you will receive a lesson that explores a critical concept of Financial Independence. There are a total of 52 lessons. If you want to learn at a quicker pace, access the Fiology material online at any time. At the end of the 52 lessons, you can feel confident that you have experienced and learned more than enough to shape your financial future and achieve Financial Independence.

Fiology uses a variety of online content that is available free on the internet. There's so much great content available that it can be overwhelming to navigate and absorb it on your own. Fiology curates this content into a framework that logically flows from one concept to the next, building your level of knowledge. This guide, as well as the activities posted in each lesson, prompts you to explore the concept of Financial Independence as it relates directly to you.

The motivation of Fiology is simply to share the message of Financial Independence. Personal profit is not a goal. If Fiology creates income or attracts donations, funds will go directly to promoting Financial Independence education, either by promoting Fiology or by supporting other organizations or projects

with the genuine mission of helping others achieve Financial Independence.

As you experience the foundation of Financial Independence via Fiology, feel free to contact me with needed updates, corrections or suggested improvements.

## Helping Hands

Once you begin this journey, you will notice that the Financial Independence community is overwhelmingly generous with their time, effort, and knowledge. I believe that we all have the ability to reach Financial Independence by our own actions. Yet there will be times when we can benefit from having an experienced Financial Independence coach in our corner.

It can be a wise decision to refer to a coach when you want reassurance, peace of mind, accountability, expertise, and motivation. If you want to explore coaching, refer to the coaches tab on the Fiology website. The coaches listed there are reputable within the Financial Independence community and have agreed to tenets that commit them to your best personal and financial interests.

*Any agreement between a client and a Financial Independence coach profiled on Fiology is entirely independent of Fiology.*

## Origin

Fiology exists out of necessity. In the past, when I introduced the concept of Financial Independence to a family member, friend, neighbor, or coworker, it always ended with me writing a list of what I considered to be the best websites and articles. Then I'd write notes on who was known for real estate, who was a frugalist, who was a minimalist, etc. I didn't know of a single site that laid out a logical step-by-step progression through the concepts of Financial Independence.

Now I can simply say, go check out fiology. com and enroll in the free weekly lessons.

I, along with thousands of others, share a passion for delivering the powerful message of Financial Independence. There are hundreds of content creators who have contributed to Fiology and there are many in the Financial Independence community who are taking action to help spread the message beyond the screens of our computers and mobile devices. This guide is part of our effort to bring the concepts of Financial Independence to the homes, classrooms, and communities where we can truly see the positive impacts of pursuing Financial Independence.

# Acknowledgements

I'd like to personally thank Maritza, Sheila, and Quentin, who continue to be gracious while I pursue this passion. My brother, Stephen, deserves much credit as he is my primary sounding board for all ideas and has helped shape Fiology since inception.

This guide would not exist without the passion and expertise of MK Williams. She led the creation of this resource with zeal and professionalism and I will be forever grateful. Her commitment to her craft will result in hundreds or thousands of people exploring Financial Independence. If you are looking for a great book to read, check out her work at 1mkwilliams.com. Thank you, MK.

The support from this community was overwhelming as this project progressed. Thank you to the generous members in the Financial Independence community who provided feedback and advice regarding the project.

The following have contributed their energy towards making this guide the best it can be: Stephen Baughier of campfi.org, Audra King of furtherjourneys.com, Kristi Arnold, Mindy Jenson of biggerpockets.com/moneyshow, Carl Jenson of 1500days. com, Nick True of mappedoutmoney.com, Doc G of diversefi.com, Kelsa Dickey of fiscalfitnessphx.com, Jillian Johnsrud of montanamoneyadventures.com, Julien and Kiersten Saunders of richandregular. com, J.D. Roth of getrichslowly.org, Doug Nordman of the-military-guide.com, Pete Adeney of mrmoneymustache.com, Tinian Crawford of diy2fi.com, Bianca DiValerio of missmazuma.com, Joel LaRosa of fi180. com, Whitney Hansen of whitneyhansen.com, Jason Williams of winningwilliams.wordpress. com, Kevin Clack of clackconsulting.com, Cody Berman of flytofi.com, Sean Mullaney of mullaneyfinancial.com, and the hundreds of others I have met face to face or online who have contributed to Fiology and share a passion for Financial Independence.

Thank you for enrolling in Fiology and spreading the powerful message of Financial Independence.

David Q. Baughier

# LESSON 1
## What Does Financial Independence Mean to Me?

Now that you have researched the term "Financial Independence" and read what it means to everyone else, what does it mean to you? Use this space to record your initial thoughts and your reasons for wanting to learn more about this topic:

To me, the term Financial Independence means...

When I am Financially Independent, my life will be...

The moment I decided I wanted to acheive Financial Independence was when...

Some of the things I always dreamed of pursuing are...

Throughout this workbook, you will have multiple opportunities to check in on how your goals are progressing. The four questions that are answered above are the most important. Cut this page out of the workbook and post it on your fridge, carry it in your wallet, or tape it to your mirror. This will serve as a reminder of why you elected to take this journey.

The scariest
moment is
just before
you start.

Stephen King

# LESSON 2
## Why FI?

Fio

"I'm no bird; and no net ensnares me: I am a free human being with an independent will."
Charlotte Bronte, Jane Eyre

At the end of the lesson was a link to "16 Reasons to Become Financially Independent" by Jillian Johnsrud of Montana Money Adventures. From this list of 16 reasons, place a check next to the reasons with which you identify most. For each of the reasons you selected, think of what impact it will have on your life. (Add any additional reasons that may be unique to your situation.)

☐ Choose where you live

☐ Start your own project

☐ Choose how long and when you travel

☐ Choose your most meaningful work

☐ Work without pay or volunteer

☐ Ability to quit if the job makes you unhappy

☐ Set boundaries at your job

☐ Improve your mental health

☐ Spend your time as you want

☐ Enjoy work because it's not for the money anymore

☐ Create space for your biggest dreams

☐ Retire when you want/need

☐ Become layoff-proof (your job won't love you back)

☐ Spend time with people who mean the most to you

☐ Other:

☐ Improve Your Physical Health

☐ Pick the amount of work you want to do

☐ Other:

Reflect on the top reasons that were selected. Why did you identify with these the most?

# LESSON 3
## How Much Do I Need?

In this lesson, we saw that the math involved in calculating the amount needed to retire is easy. The 4% Rule gives us a rough estimate: we need 25 times our annual expenses saved.

**Annual Expenses** (in retirement) \_\_\_\_\_ **×25 =** \_\_\_\_\_ amount needed

**Time to FI** \_\_\_\_\_ **+** \_\_\_\_\_ \_\_\_\_\_

current year      # years to FI      estimated FI date!

## Tracking Expenses

Knowing what the annual expenses are and calculating the amount of money to save to be FI will be difficult if you aren't already tracking your expenses. Start by writing down what you are spending. This doesn't require any changes right now, but it will help you understand how much you need to save to maintain your lifestyle.

### Common Categories

Housing
Utilities
Healthcare
Transportation
Insurance
Repairs (Home or Car)
Clothes

Groceries
Dining Out
Entertainment
Travel
Charitable Donations
Taxes

### Tools

Not a fan of pen and paper tracking? Here are just a few of the online tools available:

**Mint**
**Personal Capital**
**YNAB**
**(You Need A Budget)**
**Tiller**

# LESSON 4
## Milestones of FI

Label each milestone and list the amount and estimated time to complete. On the following pages, there are several progress charts or milestone trackers that can help you visualize your success. Pick one that works best for you and how you measure your goals.

| Milestone | Amount | Timeframe |
| --- | --- | --- |
|  |  |  |
|  |  |  |
|  |  |  |
|  |  |  |
|  |  |  |
|  |  |  |
|  |  |  |
|  |  |  |
|  |  |  |
|  |  |  |

MOTIVATION
is what gets
you started.

HABIT
is what keeps
you going.

Jim Rohn

Milestone trackers visually represent progress toward our goals. They can be very motivating! Check out a few of the ways they can be used in the following pages. Then, choose some of the milestones you want to start working toward and place them in one of the blank charts. Post it somewhere you will look at often and watch as you get closer to Financial Independence!

## Track Multiple Financial Goals:

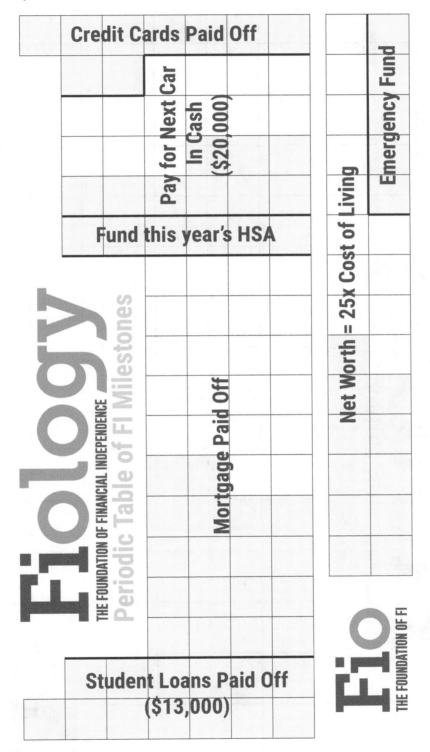

# Fiology

**THE FOUNDATION OF FINANCIAL INDEPENDENCE**

## Periodic Table of FI Milestones

**Fio**

**THE FOUNDATION OF FI**

## Track Progress Toward a Monetary Goal: (ex. save $25,000)

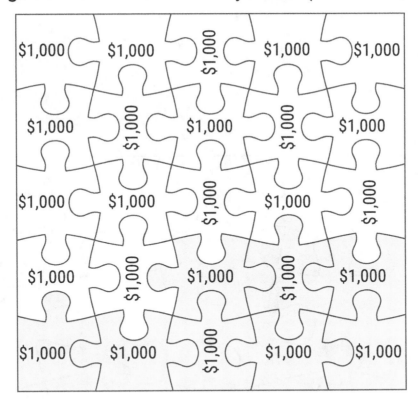

## Track Progress Toward Action Goals:

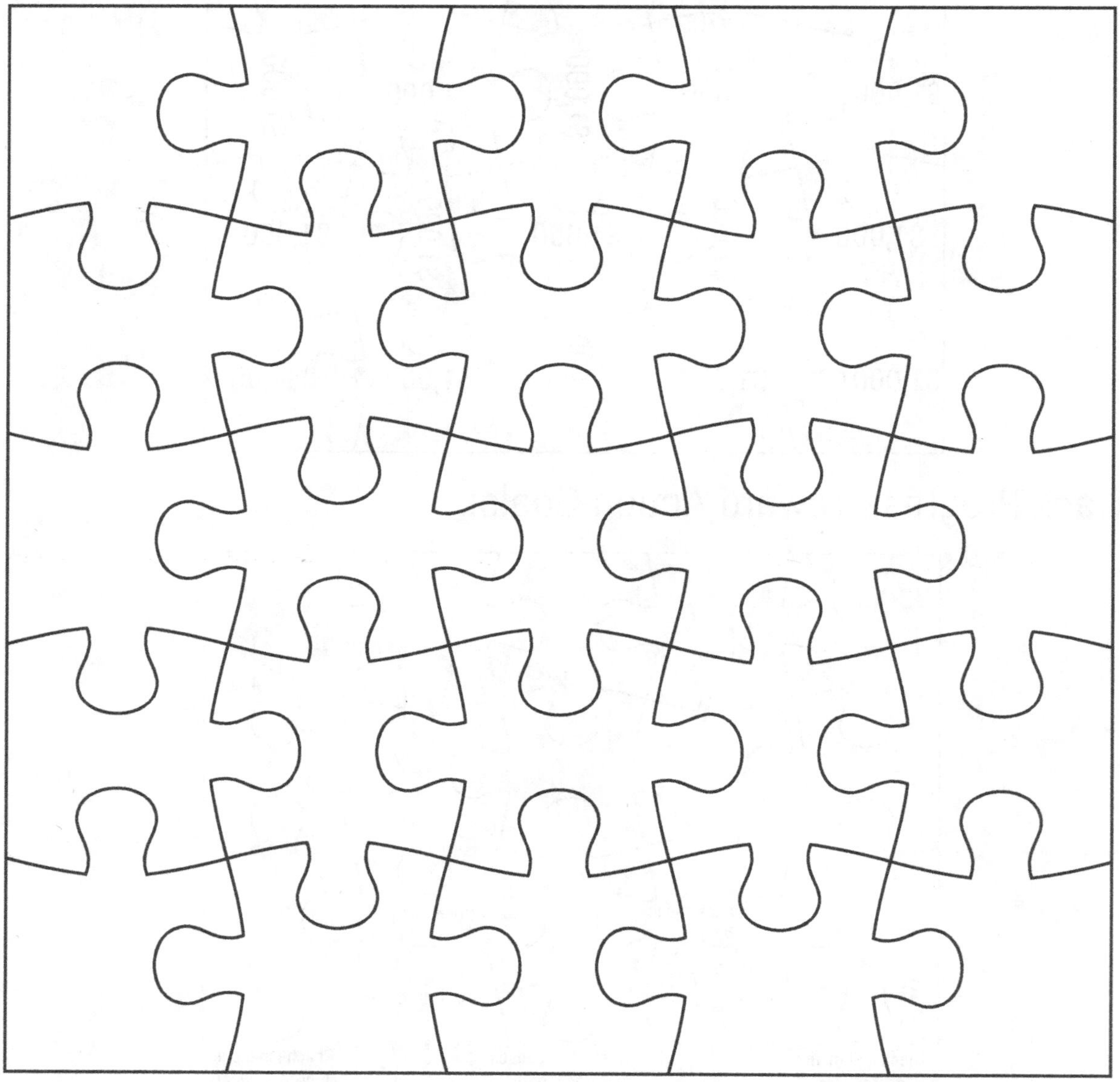

# LESSON 5

## The Big Three - Housing, Transportation, Food

We have to live somewhere, we have to get around, and we have to eat. Reflect on your current relationship with housing, transportation, and food. Can we achieve any of these elements in a more efficient way?

Take a few moments and write down your thoughts. Are your current habits in line with your values? What are your biggest concerns about making a change in each of these three areas? How much of your expenses are allocated to the big three?

*(Note: One of the articles in the lesson references that housing, transportation, and food account for roughly 60% of the average American budget in 2015.)*

_____

_____

_____

_____

_____

_____

_____

_____

_____

_____

_____

_____

_____

_____

_____

_____

_____

The price of
anything
is the amount
of life you
exchange for it.

Henry David
Thoreau

# LESSON 6
## The Miracle of Compound Interest

Having input a few scenarios online, write down one account that you can add money to starting today. Write down the original balance, the amount to add monthly, and the interest rate in this account. Refer back to this page at the end of the year to see how much the account has grown. Set a recurring reminder to check it every year to see how much was earned from interest alone.

Account:

Today's balance:

Amount to add each month:

End of year balance:

Amount I added this year:

Amount added from interest:

What will this account grow to in 20 years?

## The Double-Edged Sword

While compound interest can work for you when it comes to your savings, it can work against you on your debts. This is why some repayment advice says that you should pay off the highest interest rate debt first. Paying that one off, then the next highest interest rate, then the next, can help to prevent the debt from continuing to grow. (Note: this is referred to as the "debt avalanche" approach. Another method is the "debt snowball," where you pay off the lowest balance debt first, then roll the savings into the next and so on. Either method is effective, but the success depends on what you can put toward the debt, the interest rates on each, and what works for you.) Answer the questions below to see if the "debt avalance" method could work for you.

**If you still have outstanding debts, which one has the highest interest rate?**

**What is that rate?**

**What do you still owe?**

**What will be added each month from interest?**

**Are you motivated to pay this off ASAP?**

# LESSON 7
## Where Does All My Money Go?

Now we understand the significance of knowing where we're spending our money and have explored the tools and methods available to help us do it efficiently. It's time to reflect on your experience with budgeting and expense tracking. What surprises did you experience? What challenges did you encounter? What process changes will you make in order to stay motivated achieve your goals? Express your thoughts below.

_____

_____

_____

_____

_____

_____

_____

_____

_____

_____

_____

_____

_____

_____

_____

_____

_____

_____

A budget
is telling your
money where
to go instead
of wondering
where it went.

John C.
Maxwell

# LESSON 8
## Overcome Debt

Fio

Record the following for each of your debts:
1. Who is it with?
2. How much is left to pay?
3. When is the planned payoff date?

Cut this page out of the workbook and post it somewhere you can see it. As you pay off each debt, cross it off (or mark it complete on your Milestones of FI Tracker). Once every debt is paid off, flip the page over and proudly display that you are debt free!

| Account | Amount Remaining | Payoff Date |
|---------|------------------|-------------|
|         |                  |             |
|         |                  |             |
|         |                  |             |
|         |                  |             |
|         |                  |             |

## How Interesting...

When looking at your outstanding debts, take a look at the interest rate. Some loans may seem small; however, if the interest rates are high, you may end up paying back way more than you ever anticipated. High interest benefits the institution from which you borrowed money because they make more money. When you only make the monthly minimum payment, you are doing what you need to do. But this payment method also extends the amount of time that you will be paying off the debt, with interest. When you make additional payments, even an extra $5 to $10, you are chipping away at that balance and decreasing the principal debt and interest that you will owe later.

# Fio

# I'm Debt Free

# LESSON 9
## Retirement Account Basics

As you are reading through the lesson, you will quickly see that there is no "one-size-fits-all" option when it comes to planning your retirement. With so many options, retirement planning can be confusing. That's where Fiology comes in. It makes it easy to pick your plan. Once you have an idea of what you need to do, use this sheet to keep a clear outline of what you have selected. Use the checklists to make the most of these accounts.

## My accounts where I can defer tax payments:

☐ Money going into the account is going into an investment vehicle.

☐ I have automated the process for getting money into this account.

☐ I know the contribution limits so I don't exceed them.

## My accounts where I'll pay the tax now, but never again:

☐ Money going into the account is going into an investment vehicle.

☐ I have automated the process for getting money into this account.

☐ I know the contribution limits so I don't exceed them.

# LESSON 10
## Do My Habits Wreak Havoc?

# "An investment in knowledge pays the best interest."

### Benjamin Franklin

Habits either support our journey or impede it. In this lesson we were given the opportunity to evaluate our habits and determine if they are or are not in line with our ultimate goals. What habits will you alter or implement from this point going forward?

Benjamin Franklin perfected the art of improving his habits and his rudimentary tracker has lasted for centuries.

Using his method, mark each day that you do the positive new habits or remove old habits. Continue to track it until it becomes second nature.

## Example:

| | M | T | W | Th | F | Sa | Su |
|---|---|---|---|---|---|---|---|
| Eat Homemade Lunch | ✔ | ✔ | ✔ | ✔ | F | ✔ | ✔ |
| Give a Compliment | M | ✔ | ✔ | ✔ | F | ✔ | Su |
| Say Thank You | ✔ | ✔ | ✔ | ✔ | ✔ | ✔ | ✔ |
| Bring in Coffee from Home | ✔ | T | W | ✔ | ✔ | ✔ | ✔ |
| No Online Shopping | ✔ | ✔ | ✔ | ✔ | ✔ | ✔ | ✔ |

## Week of:

_____

| M | T | W | Th | F | S | Su |
|---|---|---|----|---|---|----|
| M | T | W | Th | F | S | Su |
| M | T | W | Th | F | S | Su |
| M | T | W | Th | F | S | Su |
| M | T | W | Th | F | S | Su |

## Week of:

_____

| M | T | W | Th | F | S | Su |
|---|---|---|----|---|---|----|
| M | T | W | Th | F | S | Su |
| M | T | W | Th | F | S | Su |
| M | T | W | Th | F | S | Su |
| M | T | W | Th | F | S | Su |

## Week of:

_____

| M | T | W | Th | F | S | Su |
|---|---|---|----|---|---|-----|

| M | T | W | Th | F | S | Su |
|---|---|---|----|---|---|-----|

_____

| M | T | W | Th | F | S | Su |
|---|---|---|----|---|---|-----|

_____

| M | T | W | Th | F | S | Su |
|---|---|---|----|---|---|-----|

_____

| M | T | W | Th | F | S | Su |
|---|---|---|----|---|---|-----|

_____

## Week of:

| M | T | W | Th | F | S | Su |
|---|---|---|----|---|---|-----|

_____

| M | T | W | Th | F | S | Su |
|---|---|---|----|---|---|-----|

_____

| M | T | W | Th | F | S | Su |
|---|---|---|----|---|---|-----|

_____

| M | T | W | Th | F | S | Su |
|---|---|---|----|---|---|-----|

_____

| M | T | W | Th | F | S | Su |
|---|---|---|----|---|---|-----|

_____

## Week of:

_____

_____

_____

_____

| M | T | W | Th | F | S | Su |
|---|---|---|----|---|---|----|
| M | T | W | Th | F | S | Su |
| M | T | W | Th | F | S | Su |
| M | T | W | Th | F | S | Su |
| M | T | W | Th | F | S | Su |

## Week of:

_____

_____

_____

_____

| M | T | W | Th | F | S | Su |
|---|---|---|----|---|---|----|
| M | T | W | Th | F | S | Su |
| M | T | W | Th | F | S | Su |
| M | T | W | Th | F | S | Su |
| M | T | W | Th | F | S | Su |

## Week of:

_____

| M | T | W | Th | F | S | Su |
|---|---|---|---|---|---|----|
| M | T | W | Th | F | S | Su |
| M | T | W | Th | F | S | Su |
| M | T | W | Th | F | S | Su |
| M | T | W | Th | F | S | Su |

## Week of:

_____

| M | T | W | Th | F | S | Su |
|---|---|---|---|---|---|----|
| M | T | W | Th | F | S | Su |
| M | T | W | Th | F | S | Su |
| M | T | W | Th | F | S | Su |
| M | T | W | Th | F | S | Su |

# Week of:

_____

_____

_____

_____

_____

| M | T | W | Th | F | S | Su |
|---|---|---|----|---|---|----|
| M | T | W | Th | F | S | Su |
| M | T | W | Th | F | S | Su |
| M | T | W | Th | F | S | Su |
| M | T | W | Th | F | S | Su |

# Week of:

_____

_____

_____

_____

_____

| M | T | W | Th | F | S | Su |
|---|---|---|----|---|---|----|
| M | T | W | Th | F | S | Su |
| M | T | W | Th | F | S | Su |
| M | T | W | Th | F | S | Su |
| M | T | W | Th | F | S | Su |

# LESSON 11
## Let Our Values Guide Our Decisions

After completing the online exercises, take a few moments to write down your values. These values should guide all of your decisions, not just the financial ones. They should guide how you spend your time, your energy, and your money.

## My Values...

_____

_____

_____

_____

_____

## I Am The Kind of Person Who...

By now, you have probably come to realize that reaching FI has more to do with your mindset than your finances. Your income and savings rate will be a product of the habits that you set. Your habits are the result of your mindset. Many in the FI community focus on their values and their core value statement. Brad Barrett, co-host of the ChooseFI podcast, said on the show that his core value statement is: "I am the kind of person who does the right thing, even when no one is watching." This is a guiding statement to help keep his decisions and actions in line with his values.

**Finish this sentence for yourself:**

"I am the kind of person who..."

_____

_____

_____

_____

_____

# LESSON 12
## The Risks of Financial Independence

In a few sentences, describe your plan to achieve Financial Independence. Will this be a simple buy and hold strategy with stocks? Will you only use real estate. Will you use a combination of the two? If you intend to incorporate something other than stocks and/or real estate, express that here.

## My FI Plan...

_____

_____

_____

_____

## The Risks to my Plan:

Detail the potential risks that you worry about. Write down a plan to counteract those risks.

| What is a Potential Risk? | How Do I Plan to Mitigate This Risk? |
| --- | --- |
| | |
| | |
| | |
| | |
| | |
| | |

If you are
always trying to
be normal
you will
never know
how amazing
you can be.

Maya Angelou

# LESSON 13
## It Pays to Be Passive

List each of your current investment accounts below. Identify the current balance and the fees associated with that account. Calculate the potential loss due to fees. If you are considering moving assets to a different account, evaluate those fees as to ensure you will pay less in fees. If you haven't established investment accounts, ensure you are aware of the fees and associated costs for the investments prior to investing.

| Account & Balance | Fees (%) | Yearly Loss (due to fees) |
|---|---|---|
|  |  |  |
|  |  |  |
|  |  |  |
|  |  |  |
|  |  |  |
|  |  |  |
|  |  |  |
|  |  |  |
|  |  |  |

# LESSON 14
## The Pension Dimension

If you have access to a Defined Benefit Plan or Pension, use this worksheet to identify and understand the specific requirements and details. No two plans are the same, so don't make informal assumptions when planning. Ensure your FI plan covers whatever gap that may exist between the money your pension will provide and the money expected for Financial Independence.

If you don't have access to a pension, you likely know someone who does. Consider using this lesson to pursue a discussion about pensions with them or take this lesson as informative and proceed to the next.

Age or date I can begin with withdrawals:

Estimated annual expenses:

Projected annual payout:

Gap between expenses and payout:

## Plan benefits:

_____

_____

## Plan requirements:

_____

_____

## Plan risks:

_____

_____

## Know Your Options

Your current career may not offer you a pension; however, you may look to make a change in the future. These are the top careers that usually offer a pension:

| | | |
|---|---|---|
| Insurance | Teaching | Local Government |
| Finance | Nursing | Military Services |
| Pharmaceuticals | Utilities | |

# LESSON 15
## Rent or Buy: What's Best for FI?

Whether you buy or rent your home, it is the place where you live. The decision to move into another rental, renew a lease, purchase a house, or sell a house should be made based on the numbers. When you remove the emotion from the decision you are more likely to make a sound financial decision. But, it can be difficult to remove emotion completely.

Review the words below and circle the ones that you associate with homeownership (both positive and negative). On the following pages, you will have the opportunity to reflect on those feelings.

Pride/"house proud"

Setting down roots

Community/belonging

Stress

"House poor"

Picket fence

Grounded/stuck

Security

Safety

Accomplishment

Forced savings

American dream

Worry
(foreclosure/repairs)

Restricted

Envy

Keeping up with the Joneses

Beginning of new traditions/memories

Use this space to journal about the emotions that come to mind when someone says, "You have to own a home," or "Renting is better, never buy."

_____

_____

_____

_____

_____

_____

_____

_____

_____

_____

Has home ownership been a goal for you and your family? What does owning a home mean to you?

_____

_____

_____

_____

_____

_____

_____

_____

_____

_____

How have your perceptions changed on this topic since beginning the Fiology course?

_____

_____

_____

_____

_____

_____

_____

_____

What concerns do you have about continuing to rent instead of owning?

_____

_____

_____

_____

_____

_____

_____

_____

_____

# LESSON 16

## Automatic Financial Independence

After learning about the benefits of automating your saving and investing, write down the first five action steps that you will take this week to automate saving or investing. What can you put aside today to make tomorrow better without having to make the decision consciously every week or month?

## My Plan to Automate Savings:

1. _____

2. _____

3. _____

4. _____

5. _____

## Automation Gone Awry...

The benefits of automation are not a secret. Many companies now operate with a subscription model where they charge customers a "small" amount every month for their services. These automated payments are often forgotten about, which is great for the bottom line of that company. The bottom line of those customers is another story.

As you evaluate automatic payments to make to yourself in the form of savings and investments, take time to look through your bank statement for any recurring payments that no longer serve you. Cancel those accounts today and watch the savings pile up!

| Account Canceled: | Frequency: | Charge: |
|---|---|---|
| _____ | _____ | _____ |
| _____ | _____ | _____ |
| _____ | _____ | _____ |
| _____ | _____ | _____ |
| _____ | _____ | _____ |

Planning our meals for the week or month not only saves us time, but also money. Not only will this help us avoid impulse spending on fast food and meals out, but it also can help us save in other ways.

When we plan, we can often identify nutritional gaps that exist in our diet and find ways to fill those gaps, improving our health and in-turn potentially saving on future healthcare.

Use the Fiology Meal Planners to map out your meals to be the most efficient fiscally and nutritionally.

# Food is an important part of a balanced diet.

# Fran Lebowitz

# Fiology

**THE FOUNDATION OF FINANCIAL INDEPENDENCE**

## WEEKLY MEAL PLANNER

| Breakfast | Lunch | Dinner | | Grocery List |
|-----------|-------|--------|---|-------------|

**M**

**T**

**W**

**Th**

**F**

**S**

**Su**

Grocery Bill:
# People X 21:

**Divide your grocery bill
by the number of meals**

Cost Per Meal =

# Fiology
## THE FOUNDATION OF FINANCIAL INDEPENDENCE
# WEEKLY MEAL PLANNER

| Grocery List | Breakfast    Lunch    Dinner |

M

T

W

Th

F

S

Su

**Grocery Bill:**
**# People X 21:**

**Divide your grocery bill**
**by the number of meals**

Cost Per Meal =

# Fiology

**THE FOUNDATION OF FINANCIAL INDEPENDENCE**

## WEEKLY MEAL PLANNER

| Breakfast    Lunch    Dinner | Grocery List |
|---|---|

**M**

**T**

**W**

**Th**

**F**

**S**

**Su**

Grocery Bill:
# People X 21:

**Divide your grocery bill
by the number of meals**

Cost Per Meal =

# Fiology

**THE FOUNDATION OF FINANCIAL INDEPENDENCE**

## WEEKLY MEAL PLANNER

| Grocery List | Breakfast    Lunch    Dinner |
|---|---|

M

T

W

Th

F

S

Su

**Grocery Bill:**
**# People X 21:**

**Divide your grocery bill by the number of meals**

Cost Per Meal =

# Fiology

**THE FOUNDATION OF FINANCIAL INDEPENDENCE**  **WEEKLY MEAL PLANNER**

| Breakfast     Lunch     Dinner | Grocery List |
|---|---|

**M**

**T**

**W**

**Th**

**F**

**S**

**Su**

Grocery Bill:
# People X 21:

**Divide your grocery bill
by the number of meals**

Cost Per Meal =

# Fiology

**THE FOUNDATION OF FINANCIAL INDEPENDENCE**

## WEEKLY MEAL PLANNER

| Grocery List | Breakfast     Lunch     Dinner |
|---|---|

M

T

W

Th

F

S

Su

**Grocery Bill:**
**# People X 21:**

**Divide your grocery bill by the number of meals**

Cost Per Meal =

# LESSON 18
## Kids and Money

What financial habits do you want your children to model? We know they mimic what we do, not just what we say. By working through the Fiology course, you are already modeling smart financial habits and that will help guide them to smarter financial choices.

What action steps will you take now to help your children learn to practice these money skills? (If you don't have any children, think about how you can model good behavior for nieces, nephews, or other young people in your life.)

Detail each habit below. How will you teach this habit to your child(ren)? How you will know when they have it mastered?

## Smart Money Habit 1:

_____

_____

_____

## Smart Money Habit 2:

_____

_____

_____

## Smart Money Habit 3:

_____

_____

_____

## Smart Money Habit 4:

_____

_____

_____

_____

Though small
was your
allowance you
saved a little
store;

And those who
save a little
shall get a
plenty more.

William
Thackeray

# LESSON 19
## Don't Evade Tax Knowledge

Find a copy of your latest tax return and review it. Everyone has to pay taxes. If you equip yourself with knowledge about the tax code, you can find opportunities to reduce your tax burden. Knowledge is more than just power in this case, you can literally save thousands of dollars just by taking some time to learn about the tax code.

AGI from last year:

Taxes due last year:

## Options available to me to reduce AGI:

☐ Retirement account payments (ex. 401k pre-tax deferrals)

☐ HSA payments (pre-tax health deferral)

☐ Other:

☐ Capital losses (tax loss harvesting)

☐ Deductions

☐ Other:

Taxes can be taxing. Many people shy away from this topic because they don't like to pay taxes and they know the penalties can be severe. Informing yourself can help you save money and help you feel empowered. What is your biggest concern when it comes to optimizing your taxes? How can you equip yourself to mitigate that risk?

_____

_____

_____

_____

_____

_____

_____

_____

_____

# LESSON 20
## Geoarbitrage

After reading through the articles in this lesson, use Dylin's method for identifying your ideal location.

### Your must-haves: (cannot live without)

_____

_____

_____

_____

### Your nice-to-haves: (ideal scenario)

_____

_____

_____

_____

### Your can-live-withouts: (there is always a compromise)

_____

_____

_____

_____

## The Cost Of Staying...

Geoarbitrage can seem like an extreme measure and to be sure, it isn't for everyone. Before dismissing the idea, find out what the cost of living is in your city. Once you know the true cost, you can understand the full impact of the choice to leave or stay.

**Your city:** _____ **Estimated cost of living:** _____

"Sometimes the people around you won't understand your journey. They don't need to, it's not for them."

Joubert Botha

How have you responded to questions about your Financial Independence goal? How do you plan to answer these questions when they come up (again) in the future? Reflect on the changes you've made and the responses you've received from others regarding your journey.

**Have you shared your journey to FI with anyone? If so, what was their response? If not, what is keepng you from sharing this information with others?**

_____

_____

_____

_____

_____

_____

_____

_____

_____

_____

_____

_____

_____

_____

**How have your perceptions about money changed over the past 21 lessons? What changes have you noticed in other areas of your life as a result of starting your journey to FI?**

_____

_____

_____

_____

_____

_____

_____

_____

_____

**Have you been able to connect with anyone else in the FI community? Has this interaction helped on your journey to FI, are you helping them on their journey?**

_____

_____

_____

_____

_____

_____

_____

_____

_____

_____

_____

# LESSON 22

## Higher Education: To Pay or Not to Pay?

If you already completed your formal education and paid for it and do not have children, you can skip this lesson. If you still have time to go to complete your degree(s) or are preparing your children for college, answer these questions to help you (or your child) determine the best option. If you are doing this exercise with your child, have them answer these questions:

By completing this degree/program/class I can...

_____

_____

_____

_____

Can I accomplish this through any other avenue?

_____

_____

_____

_____

Will I gain meaningful experience to boost my earning potential?

_____

_____

_____

_____

What will I get that I won't get anywhere else?

_____

_____

_____

_____

Education is
the key
to unlock the
golden door of
freedom.

George
Washington
Carver

# LESSON 23
## Should You Pay off Your Mortgage?

Now that you have reviewed the Mortgage Payoff Calculator online, use this worksheet to record the numbers that you discovered. How does this impact your plan to pay your mortgage?

Remaining Mortgage Balance:

Months remaining until payoff:

Additional mortgage requirements (ex. PMI):

Additional amount you can contribute to the mortgage monthly:

Interest savings from added amount:

Added savings from interest alone:

Potential added net worth if same amount was invested (assuming 8% return):

## Your Household Decision...

☐ Pay off mortgage     ☐ Invest     ☐ Both

# LESSON 24
## Net Worth ≠ Net Happiness

Reflect on the past 23 lessons. What changes have you made to your life since you began this course? Have those changes made you happier?

Use the space below to write down what makes you happy and what make you unhappy. Reflect on how you can add more of the things that make you happy, and remove the things that make you unhappy.

## What makes me happy:

_____     _____     _____

_____     _____     _____

_____     _____     _____

_____     _____     _____

I can add more of these things by:




## What makes me unhappy:

_____     _____     _____

_____     _____     _____

_____     _____     _____

_____     _____     _____

I can avoid or remove these things by:

# LESSON 25
## You "Can-Do" It Yourself!

Now that you have read through the lesson and are excited to start your first project, use the space below to track the time spent and money saved with each DIY project that you attempt. Some projects may require a technical expert or may take too much time to complete. Others you may be able to look up on YouTube to learn how to do it yourself. Use this tracking document to see how you have come out ahead by tackling each project yourself:

| Project | Cost of Materials | Time Spent |
| --- | --- | --- |
| | | |
| | | |
| | | |
| | | |
| | | |
| | | |
| | | |
| | | |
| | | |

# LESSON 26

## Withdrawing Funds Before Age 59½

Depending on your estimated time to reach FI and your individual plan to retire, you may need to access the funds in your tax-advantaged retirement accounts before the age of 59 1/2. If your plan has you retiring after that age, skip ahead. If your plan has you retiring prior to this age, use this worksheet to help you plan.

Estimated age at retirement:

Years until you can withdraw:

Estimated annual expenses in FI:

Amount needed prior to 59½
(line 2 × line 3):

Tactics I will leverage to access funds prior to 59½:

_____

_____

## Required Minimum Distribution

The U.S. Government set the age of 59 1/2 to be able to withdraw funds from tax-advantaged retirement accounts. We learned about the loopholes in this rule in lesson 26. For those of you who are thinking that you have so much saved and will work long enough that you won't have to touch these funds for a very long time, keep in mind that the U.S. Government also set a **required minimum distribution.** Effectively, you can't keep your money in the tax-advantaged accounts forever. At the age of 70 1/2, you have to start withdrawing the money in those accounts (there are some rules around this that you should familiarize yourself with).

Keep in mind that when you withdraw funds from a tax-advantaged account you will be required to pay tax on that income. This fact should factor into your FI tax planning.

Happiness is
not the mere
possession of
money;
it lies in the joy
of achievement,
in the thrill of
effort.

Franklin D.
Roosevelt

# LESSON 27
## Mindfulness

The journey to FI involves much more than budgeting and saving. Many people on this path discover that their mindset shifts as they find ways to improve all aspects of their lives. Take this time to reflect on your mindfulness practice. Have you started a practice? What changes have you noted in your ability to focus on the things that mean the most to you?

# LESSON 28
## Join Forces for FI

Money conversations with a partner can be challenging. Complete this worksheet to verify alignment and identify differences of attitudes towards money. This can serve as an outline for valuable discussion. No two people agree on all things one hundred percent of the time. If you discover you become passionate about any differences, ask yourself why you might feel so strongly about it. Is that difference more important than the love and respect you have for the other person? You and your partner are in this together, consideration must always remain a priority in working through differences on the FI journey.

My biggest financial concern is:

_____

_____

Their biggest financial concern is:

_____

_____

I would prefer to spend money on:

_____

_____

They would prefer to spend money on:

_____

_____

Financial goals we have agreed on and committed to together:

_____

_____

_____

_____

# LESSON 29
## Cut the Cords That Tie Us Down

Use this tracking sheet to log the amount of time that you spend watching TV. We all enjoy our shows, but standard cable packages can be expensive. With the dawn of multiple online streaming services, there could be a less expensive option that can help accelerate your path to FI.

TV Hours:

Week 1 _____

Week 2 _____

Week 3 _____

Week 4 _____

Week 5 _____

| | | |
|---|---|---|
| ☐ Write a list of my "must-have" shows or sports. | ☐ Compare streaming cost with standard cable cost. | ☐ Investigate cable internet and use high speed internet to watch shows. |
| ☐ Research other services that stream my favorite shows. | ☐ Calculate # of hours watching cable to get same per hour value from streaming. | ☐ Cancel cable service. Invest the savings. |

## Personal Finance Is Personal

While cutting the cord on cable can be an easy way to save on costs for some, it may be a more difficult decision for others. You know your situation and what you are willing to do. The beauty of Financial Independence is that you can make the choices that are the best for you. Many people on the path to FI constantly challenge themselves to question the assumptions that guide many in our society.

Give the television a break and see if it could work for you. If you find that this is something you can't live without, then you can say that you tried and plan for the cost in your FI budget. Keep in mind that when you withdraw funds from a tax-advantaged account you will be required to pay tax on that income. This fact should factor into your FI tax planning.

# LESSON 30
## The FI-brary

"The only thing that you absolutely have to know, is the location of the library."

Albert Einstein

As we look to cut costs without sacrificing the things you love, the library can be an amazing resource. Review the resources at the local library and check off which ones are available. Make a plan to go this weekend to see the benefits for yourself.

| | | |
|---|---|---|
| ☐ Books | ☐ Museum passes | ☐ Classes and workshops |
| ☐ Movies | ☐ Language guides | ☐ Access to E-learning |
| ☐ Music | ☐ Genealogy resources | ☐ Musical instruments |
| ☐ Digital loans | ☐ Storytime for children | ☐ Tools |
| ☐ Seeds | ☐ Career resources | ☐ Tax resources |
| ☐ Other: | ☐ Other: | ☐ Other: |
| ☐ Other: | ☐ Other: | ☐ Other: |

# LESSON 31
## Don't Cell Yourself Short

Now that you are aware of Mobile Virtual Network Operators (MVNOs) and the ability to save significantly on your cell phone plan, go through this worksheet to help determine what will work best for you.

## Step 1: How much do you need?

Those of us on the path to FI track everything. We do this so that we can ensure we are getting the most value from how we spend our time and money. Look at your current plan. How much data are you allotted monthly and how much do you use? Could you scale down your plan or even eliminate cellular data altogether?

Average data used in past 3 months:

Desired data use in next 3 months:

## Step 2: Who looks at your phone?

Throughout our community, there is a place for everyone. There's even a place for those who rush out to get the latest and greatest technology when it is released. If it brings them that much value, then of course they should have what they value. Do you feel this way about your phone? Do you need the newest model with the most advanced features? You're the person who looks at your phone the most. It needs to be right for you, not for anyone else.

Cost to purchase phone outright:

Cost to lease my phone:

Features I need:

_____     _____     _____

_____     _____     _____

Features I want:

_____     _____     _____

_____     _____     _____

# LESSON 32
## Whole, Term, or No Life Insurance?

## "Please think about your legacy, because you are writing it every day."

### Gary Vaynerchuk

Most insurance covers us "just in case" something happens. But life insurance provides financial security for something that we know without a doubt will happen. We will all die one day. While we plan and take action to live a long and healthy life, insurance can provide financial stability while we are still working toward FI. Use the space below to list out what you want to leave behind. Is it money to fund your children's college expenses? Is it a property for your spouse? Do you want to leave behind memories and positively impact your community? What you plan for now is what you will leave behind.

**What will you leave behind financially, emotionally, or otherwise?**

_____

_____

_____

_____

_____

_____

_____

_____

_____

_____

_____

_____

_____

_____

# LESSON 33
## Health Insurance

Following the guidance from this lesson, look up your current coverage and compare that to another available plan. We often look at this once a year when our plans are up for renewal, but this information is important year-round. Evaluate your options so that you can find the right plan for your needs and budget accordingly.

| 1. Current Plan | Notes | 2. Alternative Plan |
|---|---|---|
| Monthly Cost: | | Monthly Cost: |
| Annual Cost: | | Annual Cost: |
| Deductibles | | Deductibles |
| Copays: | | Copays: |
| Out of pocket maximum: | | Out of pocket maximum: |
| Prescriptions: | | Prescriptions: |
| Other considerations: | | Other considerations: |

Once you have
enough money,
it's not about
the money.

David Q.
Baughier

# LESSON 34
## Reinforce FI with Rentals

Investing in real estate is a proven tool of choice for many who have learned the basic principles and understand the associated risks and how to mitigate them. Question your current beliefs that may be based on stories of others who tried and failed. Learn enough from those that have found a level of success to feel confident about your decision. Think seriously about how rental properties may fit into your overall FI plan. You may find it's worth pursuing or you may decide it just isn't a good fit.

In the space below, write down notes and questions you have for deeper exploration on rental real estate.

_____

_____

_____

_____

_____

_____

_____

_____

_____

_____

_____

_____

_____

_____

# LESSON 35
## Travel Reward Yourself

There is usually a lot of excitement around travel rewards. Who doesn't want an all expenses covered trip to a tropical island or the trip of a lifetime to another continent? Those trips are achievable with travel rewards, but don't forget about the little trips, too!

Review the list below and check off the types of trips that you would like to be able to take. Having a vision and a reason to start gathering travel rewards will help you acheive your goal. (Add on a few of your own as well)

☐ Bucket list trip

☐ Attend a reunion

☐ Getaway with spouse/partner

☐ Visit family

☐ Attend a distant wedding

☐ Fly in for a funeral

☐ Family vacation

☐ Participate in a mission trip

☐ Attend a retreat

☐ Other:

☐ Other:

☐ Other:

## A Caution On Credit

This lesson has a disclaimer about using credit card bonuses to generate travel rewards. If you carry credit card debt and are not in the habit of paying off the balance each month, then this strategy may not be for you at this time. Once you have established those habits and repaired any credit damage, revisit this lesson.

These benefits are always evolving, you can stay up to date on the latest news online. Many people on the path to FI have discovered this benefit and are happy to share their experience and tips with others.

# LESSON 36
## Decluttering the Home and Self

Now that we have covered the fundamentals of FI, it is easy to see that it really isn't about the money. It's about knowing what is important to you and focusing your time and energy there. Once you know what your priorities are, it is easy to declutter and donate items that no longer serve you (or that tie up valuable space and time).

Take on the 30 Day Challenge and log your progress here. It's easy to start (give away one item on day one, two items on day two), but it will become more challenging as the month continues.

Day 1    _____

Day 2    _____    _____

Day 3    _____    _____    _____

Day 4    _____    _____    _____    _____

Day 5    _____    _____    _____    _____
         _____

Day 6    _____    _____    _____    _____
         _____    _____

Day 7    _____    _____    _____    _____
         _____    _____    _____

Day 8    _____    _____    _____    _____
         _____    _____    _____

Day 9    _____    _____    _____    _____
         _____    _____    _____    _____
         _____

Day 10 _____ _____ _____ _____

_____ _____ _____ _____

_____ _____

Day 11 _____ _____ _____ _____

_____ _____ _____ _____

_____ _____ _____ _____

Day 12 _____ _____ _____ _____

_____ _____ _____ _____

_____ _____ _____ _____

Day 13 _____ _____ _____ _____

_____ _____ _____ _____

_____ _____ _____ _____

_____

Day 14 _____ _____ _____ _____

_____ _____ _____ _____

_____ _____ _____ _____

_____ _____

Day 15 _____ _____ _____ _____

_____ _____ _____ _____

_____ _____ _____ _____

_____ _____ _____

Day 16 _____ _____ _____ _____

_____ _____ _____ _____

_____ _____ _____ _____

_____ _____ _____ _____

**Day 17** _____  _____  _____  _____

_____  _____  _____  _____

_____  _____  _____  _____

_____  _____  _____  _____

_____

**Day 18** _____  _____  _____  _____

_____  _____  _____  _____

_____  _____  _____  _____

_____  _____

**Day 19** _____  _____  _____  _____

_____  _____  _____  _____

_____  _____  _____  _____

_____  _____  _____  _____

**Day 20** _____  _____  _____  _____

_____  _____  _____  _____

_____  _____  _____  _____

_____  _____  _____  _____

**Day 21** _____  _____  _____  _____

_____  _____  _____  _____

_____  _____  _____  _____

_____  _____  _____  _____

_____

**Day 22** _____  _____  _____  _____

_____  _____  _____  _____

_____  _____  _____  _____

_____  _____  _____  _____

_____  _____

**Day 23** _____  _____  _____  _____

_____  _____  _____  _____

_____  _____  _____  _____

_____  _____  _____  _____

_____  _____  _____

**Day 24** _____  _____  _____  _____

_____  _____  _____  _____

_____  _____  _____  _____

_____  _____  _____  _____

_____  _____  _____  _____

**Day 25** _____  _____  _____  _____

_____  _____  _____  _____

_____  _____  _____  _____

_____  _____  _____  _____

_____  _____  _____  _____

_____

**Day 26** _____ _____ _____ _____

_____ _____ _____ _____

_____ _____ _____ _____

_____ _____ _____ _____

_____ _____ _____ _____

_____ _____ _____ _____

_____ _____

**Day 27** _____ _____ _____ _____

_____ _____ _____ _____

_____ _____ _____ _____

_____ _____ _____ _____

_____ _____ _____ _____

_____ _____ _____ _____

_____ _____ _____

**Day 28** _____ _____ _____ _____

_____ _____ _____ _____

_____ _____ _____ _____

_____ _____ _____ _____

_____ _____ _____ _____

_____ _____ _____ _____

_____ _____ _____ _____

Day 29 _____ _____ _____ _____
        _____ _____ _____ _____
        _____ _____ _____ _____
        _____ _____ _____ _____
        _____ _____ _____ _____
        _____ _____ _____ _____
        _____ _____ _____ _____
        _____

Day 30 _____ _____ _____ _____
        _____ _____ _____ _____
        _____ _____ _____ _____
        _____ _____ _____ _____
        _____ _____ _____ _____
        _____ _____ _____ _____
        _____ _____ _____ _____
        _____ _____

Now that you have had a chance to practice decluttering for 30 days, reflect on the process.
Was it easier than you expected or more difficult? What kind of things were the most effortless
to let go of? Which ones were the hardest? What did you learn during the past 30 days?

_____

_____

_____

_____

_____

_____

_____

_____

Someone is
sitting in the
shade today
because
someone
planted a tree
a long time ago.

Warren Buffet

# LESSON 37

## Car Buying While Driving Towards FI

It's no surprise that the Big 3 - Food, Housing, and Transportation - come with a lot of emotions. Whether it was instilled by our familiies, friends, or our surroundings, we often have strong opinions on these topics. When you think about buying a new car or a pre-owned car, what comes to mind?

Use these word associations to help you start to process your emotions on the topic. Once you do that, you can make a clear-minded decision on your next car purchase.

"I've made it"                           Another payment

                    Hidden costs

Deserve a new car/                       "Get from A to B"
I work hard for it

                    Speed

Style                                    Power

                    Safety

Accidents                                Stuck in traffic

                    American dream

Worry                                    Family car/ plan to
(damages/repairs)                        hand down

                    Envy

Keeping up with                          Don't want a lemon, but
the Joneses                              can't afford luxury

**Use this space to journal about the emotions that come to mind when someone says, "You have to buy new" or "You should never buy a new car."**

_____

_____

_____

_____

_____

_____

_____

_____

_____

**What goals or dreams have you had around the type of car that you would own? Is this part of your identity?**

_____

_____

_____

_____

_____

_____

_____

_____

_____

_____

_____

# LESSON 38
## The Prenup Proposal

You and your partner are in love and will never need a prenup because you are never going to get divorced. One hundred percent of couples believe this when they get married, only 50 percent are correct. While we will continue to believe in the strength of our relationship, it is wise to plan for the unfortunate possibility that, at some point, the decision may be made to part ways. You may find that this planning brings you closer together and strengthens your relationship.

Use the questions below to guide your discussion:

What, if any, financial gains were earned before our marriage? Do we want to protect any or are these shared?

What assets should be protected for the children? Can we agree on what they will get in the case of a divorce?

Who will own the revenue and intellectual property from an individually-owned business? Did we build this together?

Did we have to pay off debt together? Was this our debt or did one person bring more debt to the relationship? How would we compensate the other to account for this payment?

What are the laws in our state? How would the state divide our property if it was up to a court to decide?

Who is likely to retire first? Who has contributed/ been able to contribute to retirement savings? What agreements did we make as a family about working and saving and how would we want to protect each other?

## All Marriages End

Fifty percent of all marriages end in divorce, the other in death. Not all of us will have a fairy-tale ending from The Notebook and pass at the same time as our spouse.

While these are never fun conversations to have, what is your plan should you or your spouse die? Will you and your family be able to maintain your current lifestyle? Does your partner have access to all of your accounts? Take a few moments to store important information where your partner can find it.

# LESSON 39
## Side Hustle Up!

Now that we know the power that a side hustle can have, take a few moments to write down some of the side hustles that you think can work for you.

## My Side Hustle Ideas:

_____   _____   _____

_____   _____   _____

_____   _____   _____

_____   _____   _____

Not only can a side hustle generate income, but it can be fun. Having a self-sustaining project outside of the 9-to-5 can give you a renewed sense of purpose. This can also be something that you can focus on when you retire so that you know how you will spend your time. Take a few moments to write down what your ideal day would look like: **what would you work on or create?**

_____

_____

_____

_____

_____

_____

_____

_____

_____

_____

_____

The extra work for this lesson can't be done in a workbook. For this, you need to expand your network. Join one of the many Facebook groups for people on the path to FI. Attend one of the local meet-ups in your area. Find like-minded people to talk to about your journey.

Never doubt
that a small
group of thoughtful,
committed citizens
can change the world;

indeed, it's
the only thing
that ever has.

Margaret Mead

# LESSON 41
## Who is Your FI Mentor?

We know we need guidance and mentors to help us develop and grow. Think back to your school days. Who was that teacher, coach, or family friend that helped you grow?

Answer the questions below to discover who might serve as your perfect mentor. Then ask that person. They will likely be honored to support you and your goals.

## Questions To Help You Find A Financial Mentor:

Who is already in your circle of acquaintances?

Of the people that come to mind as potential mentors, do they have a teaching personality? Have they already helped in an informal way?

How do you plan to broach the subject? Can you think through what the benefit will be for them?

Do you identify with their story? What do you share in common and where do you differ?

Is this person generous with their time? What value can you give back to them?

Can you listen and take advice from this person?

Who can **you** help on their journey?

## Thank Goodness For The Internet

While meeting face-to-face may be the image that we picture when we think of "mentoring," that may not always be practical. With the development of the FI community and the availability of communication via the internet, it has never been easier to meet and connect with a financial mentor, even if they are far away.

# LESSON 42
## Opportunity Costs

Instead of beating yourself up over past decisions, focus on big decisions that loom on the horizon for you. Maybe it is a new job opportunity, maybe you know that you will need to replace a car within the next year. Whether it will take up a considerable amount of money or time, map out the opportunity costs associated with that decision to help you make the best of each situation.

### Opportunity Cost 1

If I choose _____ then I will give up:

_____    _____    _____

_____    _____    _____

(Circle the items that align with your values.)

### Opportunity Cost 2

If I choose _____ then I will give up:

_____    _____    _____

_____    _____    _____

(Circle the items that align with your values.)

### Opportunity Cost 1

If I choose _____ then I will give up:

_____    _____    _____

_____    _____    _____

(Circle the items that align with your values.)

# LESSON 43
## FI-losophy - Stoicism

While not everyone is jumping to practice stoicism, those on the path to FI have seen the many benefits of embracing this philosophy. In our day-to-day lives we are inundated with stimuli. Marketers are constantly trying to prey on our emotions to drive their sales. We can steel ourselves against this and other distractions by practicing stoicism. One way to do this is to practice voluntary discomfort. If we can get through these exercises and keep our minds focused, then surely our minds can stay focused through any distractions that life throws at us.

## Ways to Practice Voluntary Discomfort:

☐ Fast for a day

☐ Skip your A.M. coffee/tea

☐ Sleep on the floor

☐ Turn off the A/C in the summer

☐ Take a cold shower

☐ Bike to work

☐ Exercise in the morning

☐ Leave the heat off in the winter

☐ Take a walk in the rain

## A Philosophy To Embrace

There is a reason that this philosophy has endured the centuries, it works! If practicing voluntary discomfort is too much, start by reading and meditating on these quotes from the great stoic philosophers:

Fate leads the willing, and drags along the reluctant.
- Seneca, Letters from a Stoic

We should always be asking ourselves: "Is this something that is, or is not, in my control?"
- Epictetus, Enchiridion

If you are pained by any external thing, it is not this thing that disturbs you, but your own judgment about it. And it is in your power to wipe out this judgment now.
- Marcus Aurelius, Meditations

Any goal
worth
achieving
involves an
element
of risk.

Dean Karnazes

# LESSON 44
## Sequence of Returns Risk

As we get into the final few weeks of the Fiology lessons, much of what you have learned earlier will come into play. The topics addressed in this lesson are vital to success in retirement. If you plan to live off the returns that your investment accounts can generate, a year where returns are down can significantly impact your plans.

After reading and reviewing the content, use this space to jot down the questions specific to your retirement plans. Use these as a guide when you continue to research answers. There is no one-size-fits-all approach. Doing your research will help you feel confident that you have selected the right path for you. Track your questions and the resources that have been the most helpful. .

**My questions on sequence of returns risk...**

_____

_____

_____

_____

_____

_____

**Helpful resources on sequence of returns risk...**

_____

_____

_____

_____

_____

_____

_____

# LESSON 45
## Real Estate Investment Trusts

Earlier in this course, we looked at the pros and cons of owning a home and owning rental properties. For those who want to diversify their portfolio with real estate but aren't interested in property management, REITs can be a great opportunity. For those who have no interest in owning any kind of real estate, individual properties or otherwise, that is OK, too.

Answer the questions below to help determine if investing in REITs is worth pursuing as part of your FI portfolio.

**Do you think you may want to invest in REITs?  If yes, how will they support your financial goals?**

_____

_____

_____

_____

_____

_____

_____

_____

_____

_____

_____

_____

_____

_____

_____

_____

**How will adding REITs to your portfolio likely affect your long-term returns and risk profile?**

_____

_____

_____

_____

_____

_____

_____

_____

_____

**What is the likely overall difference of choosing to include a REIT over simply continuing to contribute to a low-cost broad market index fund?**

_____

_____

_____

_____

_____

_____

_____

_____

_____

_____

# LESSON 46
## One More Year Syndrome

As the FI finish line gets closer, take a moment to reflect on the emotions tied to this action. Getting to your FI number is math, but pulling the trigger on leaving the workforce can be challenging. That is why so many continue to work for just "one more year."

Review the words below and circle the ones with which you identify. This exercise will help you to do the mental work of preparing for your retirement (early or standard).

"I'm outta here"

Nervous

"What if I get bored?"

"I'm finally going to do _____"

"After this project Is completed"

Optimism

"What if..."

"They need me"

"I don't know what I'll do with my time"

Restlessness

Excitement

Worry

"I've already got my to-do list"

Adventure

"Can't find a good replacement"

"Take this job and..."

"Well, if I stay another month I get..."

# LESSON 47
## Dream Big

No, this isn't a misprint. The first step to thinking big is imagining the possibilities. Now that you are on the path to FI and money will no longer be a burden, what will you do in FI? What is your big dream? Use this space to write, sketch, doodle, whatever you need to do in order to imagine the possibilities of a life free to pursue what you want.

# LESSON 48
## Caring for Aging Parents

Before you have a tough conversation with your parents, be sure that you can answer these questions for yourself. The transition from adult-child to caregiver (physically or financially) is tough for both parties. Review the questions posed in this lesson. Set yourself and your future caregivers up for success.

**Have you taken care of your Financial Independence? Does your plan account for increased costs as you age?**

_____

_____

_____

_____

_____

_____

_____

_____

_____

_____

_____

_____

_____

_____

_____

_____

_____

_____

_____

**What would it mean to have the time and money to be able to spend time with your family? How are you planning for this?**

_____

_____

_____

_____

_____

_____

_____

_____

_____

**When the time comes, will your caregivers be able to take over your financial affairs?**

_____

_____

_____

_____

_____

_____

_____

_____

_____

_____

_____

# LESSON 49
## Social Security

Social Security may or may not be there for us when we retire. Before we dismiss this potential source of income in retirement, we need to evaluate our assumptions about it. As you've seen over the past 48 lessons, the FI community questions assumptions in order to make the best decision for their individual plan. After you've logged your assumptions, take time to do some research on these topics.

Use the official online calculator: https://www.ssa.gov/OACT/quickcalc/

## I think I'll get this much monthly from SS:

## With SS, I'll only need to save:

## I think Social Security will be:

☐ Fully funded through my retirement

☐ Something I'll have access to for a few years, but it won't last

☐ Long gone by the time I can withdraw

## Don't Retire Too Soon!

Don't pull the trigger too soon! As of 2019, you still need at least 40 credits with the Social Security Administration (SSA) to even become eligible to receive benefits. These credits are calculated quarterly, which means you need 10 years (with four quarters each) of credits. While it may seem far-fetched that someone could retire in less than 10 years, we have examples of this in the Financial Independence community.

The SSA doesn't account for early retirees in many of their calculators. Most assume that you will continue to work and contribute a similar amount until you reach retirement age. Keep this in mind as you run the calculators as part of this exercise.

# LESSON 50
## The Dynamic Journey

Throughout this course, we've asked you to stop and reflect on your thoughts and feelings around certain topics. As we near the end of the course and you have all of the skills necessary to continue on your path to FI, how do you think you've grown?

After completing this page, go back to the first pages and review your answers to the questions in lesson one. Have your goals and dreams remained the same? Have you already reached them? How has your journey been unique?

To me, the term Financial Independence means...

When I am Financially Independent, my life will be...

The moment I decided I wanted to acheive Financial Independence was when...

Some of the things I always dreamed of pursuing are...

# LESSON 51
## Living the FI Life

Whether you have reached FI by the end of this course or if you need to return to it a bit later, congratulations! If you are doing this exercise you have set a date on the calendar to retire. Whatever your age, this is an exciting time. In this lesson, we saw that those who were successful at reaching FI didn't suddenly turn into couch potatoes and cease being productive in their retirement. Far from it, they set goals for what they wanted to accomplish with their time.

In this exercise, create a list of goals or tasks that you want to accomplish in the first year of your retired life. Rip it out and stick it on your refrigerator so you can cross off these items as you accomplish them. You don't have to wait until you are Financially Independent to start living the life you design for yourself, start accomplishing these things now if you can.

## My FI List:

| | | |
|---|---|---|
| _____ | _____ | _____ |
| _____ | _____ | _____ |
| _____ | _____ | _____ |
| _____ | _____ | _____ |
| _____ | _____ | _____ |
| _____ | _____ | _____ |
| _____ | _____ | _____ |
| _____ | _____ | _____ |
| _____ | _____ | _____ |
| _____ | _____ | _____ |
| _____ | _____ | _____ |
| _____ | _____ | _____ |
| _____ | _____ | _____ |

Similar to the last day of school in our younger years, this final lesson is a celebration of your accomplishments.

Your FI journey certainly doesn't stop here. You will continue to expand your knowledge and become more confident and competent in all things Financial Independence. You'll continue to receive lessons in your inbox to reinforce the content and receive updated content over time.

Now that you have had the chance to read articles from a wide-ranging group of bloggers in the FI space, continue to support them. Get out there and go to a local meet-up or a CampFI event. Share the word about this program with others who can benefit from these principles.

Congratulations and thank you for sharing your journey with Fiology!

---

# The need for connection and community is primal, as fundamental as air, water, food.

## Dean Ornish

# NOTES